I'm Reading About

The STATUE OF LIBERTY

GALLOPADE

by Carole Marsh

Printed and Manufactured in Peachtree City, GA., USA www.gallopade.com

Book design: Susan Van Denhende

Editor: Janice Baker

Photo Credits: Cover: ssviluppo/Bigstock.com. Page 3: Robert Voight//Bigstock.com. Page 5: Zigi/Bigstock.com. Page 6: United States Mint. Pages 9 and 28: Holbox/Bigstock.com. Page 11: dennizn/Bigstock.com; 11A: Napoleon Sarony. Page 12: iclipart.com. Page 13A: National Park Service; 13B: Nadar/gettyimages.co.uk. Page 15: Kent Weakley/Bigstock.com; 15A: Library of Congress. Page 17A&C: Library of Congress; 17B: http://nozoma.typepad.com. Page 18: bennymarty/Bigstock.com. Page 20A: Wikimedia Commons; 20B: Library of Congress. Page 22A: Museum of the City of New York; 22B: sylv1rob1/Bigstock.com. Page 24: kropic/Bigstock.com. Page 26: Frank Leslie's Illustrated Newspaper, Library of Congress. Page 28A: New York Historical Society; 28B: Lewis Hine, Google Art Project. Pages 30A: National Park Service; 30B&C: Library of Congress. Page 32A: Waxen/Bigstock.com; 32B: National Park Service. Page 34: gary718/Bigstock.com.

The Statue of Liberty
is a great place to visit!

What is so special about
the Statue of Liberty?

Let's read about it and see!

INTRODUCTION

The Statue of Liberty is an enormous statue.
It stands on Liberty Island in New York Harbor
in New York City.

The Statue of Liberty is a symbol of freedom
to people around the world!
She represents Libertas, the Roman goddess of liberty.

The statue's original name was
"Liberty Enlightening the World."

Statue of Liberty

LOCATION

Liberty Island is located in New York Harbor.
It is one of the busiest harbors in the United States!
Ships come to New York from around the world.

New York was one of the original 13 colonies.
It became a state in 1788.
It was the 11th state to join
the United States of America!

New York
Here it is!

STATUE

The Statue of Liberty is huge—151 feet tall!
She is often called "Lady Liberty."
The statue is made of copper sheets attached
to a metal framework.

In her left hand, she holds a tablet with the date
July 4, 1776—the date of America's independence!
In her right hand she holds a torch.
It represents the light of freedom!

The statue was originally brown.
The copper turned green over the years.

Lady Liberty

HISTORY

The Statue of Liberty was a gift from France.
In 1865, a group of Frenchmen decided to build a monument to American freedom.
They also wanted to show their friendship to the U.S.

A sculptor named Frédéric Auguste Bartholdi designed the monument.
Bartholdi wanted to deliver the statue by July 4, 1876—America's 100th birthday!

Gift from France

Frédéric Bartholdi

DESIGN

An engineer named Gustave Eiffel helped Bartholdi. He designed the framework for the statue. He made sure the statue could withstand high winds and extreme weather!

Both France and America had roles in the project:

- The French would build the statue.
- The Americans would build a pedestal for it.

Gustave Eiffel also designed the Eiffel Tower in Paris.

Statue's Design

"Skeleton" of Statue

Gustave Eiffel

Bartholdi used about 300 thin copper sheets for the outside of the statue.
Workers hammered the copper sheets into different shapes.

Then, the sheets were mounted onto the framework.
The sheets were very thin—about the thickness of two pennies put together!

Building Process

PARTS & PIECES

The Statue of Liberty was actually built in pieces.
The statue was completed in June 1884,
and stood in Paris for about a year.

The statue was taken apart for shipment to the U.S.
There were 350 pieces packed in 214 crates!

The Statue of Liberty arrived in New York Harbor
in June 1885.
But she had to wait for a while
because her pedestal was not ready.

Built in Pieces

Facing the Sea

The pedestal for the Statue of Liberty
was built on Bedloe's Island in New York Harbor.
The pedestal was located inside Fort Wood,
an old army base.
Fort Wood was built in the shape of a star.

The pedestal points southeast.
That way, the statue faces ships entering the harbor
from the Atlantic Ocean.
The Statue of Liberty greets all newcomers!

Bedloe's Island was officially renamed
"Liberty Island" in 1956.

PEDESTAL

Assembling the Statue

ASSEMBLY

When the pedestal was finished in 1886, it was time to put the Statue of Liberty back together!

Many of the construction workers were new immigrants to the United States. First, they put the framework together. Then, they attached the copper covering.

The statue's face was the last section built. Workers left a veil over the face until the statue was dedicated.

Dedication Celebration

celebration!

Flag of France

DEDICATION

The Statue of Liberty was dedicated
on October 28, 1886.
It was a rainy day, but people were excited!
A million New Yorkers attended a parade to celebrate.
President Grover Cleveland was there, too!

The sculptor Bartholdi hid in the statue's head.
He pulled a cord to remove the French flag
over Lady Liberty's face.
The crowd cheered and gunshot salutes rang out!

France's centennial gift was dedicated
10 years after America's 100th birthday.

Large Lady

BY THE NUMBERS

The Statue of Liberty is a very LARGE lady!

- She stands 305 feet tall from ground to torch tip.
- Her right arm is 42 feet long.
- Her nose is over 4 feet long.
- Her head is 10 feet wide.
- Her index finger is 8 feet long!

Welcome to America

IMMIGRANTS

Before airplanes were invented,
immigrants traveled to America on ships.
Millions of them sailed across the Atlantic Ocean
to enter the U.S. in New York City.

The Statue of Liberty became an important landmark
as immigrants entered New York Harbor.
Many of them cried when they saw it!
Lady Liberty was a symbol of freedom, hope,
and a new life!

A lovely lady standing tall
represents freedom for one and all!

Promise of Liberty

Emma Lazarus

Immigrant Family

POEM

A famous poem was written about the Statue of Liberty: "The New Colossus," by Emma Lazarus.

Today, the words of the poem are engraved on a bronze plaque inside the pedestal. Several famous lines welcome immigrants to America:

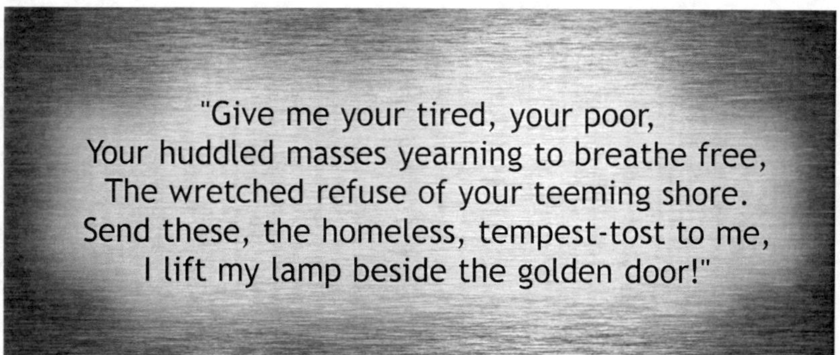

Repairing the Statue

PRESERVATION

The Statue of Liberty is pounded by heat, cold, wind, and rain every day of the year. In the 1980s, experts noticed that the statue was showing signs of wear and tear.

The National Park Service closed the statue for two years to make repairs to Lady Liberty:

- Much of the statue's "skeleton" was replaced.
- Holes in the copper covering were repaired.
- The torch was completely replaced.

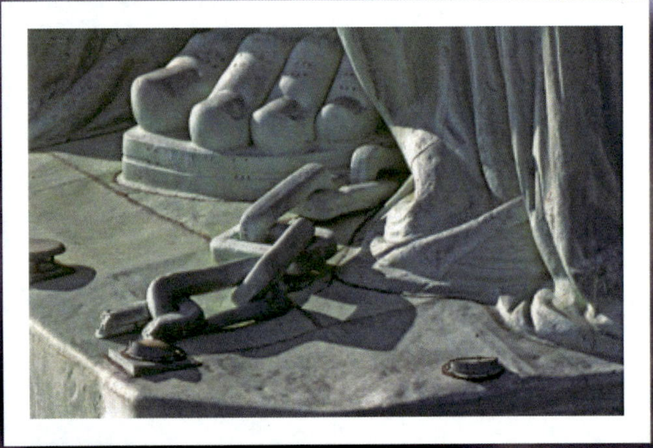

Astounding Statue

DID YOU KNOW?

Read more fascinating facts about the Statue of Liberty:

- Lightning often hits the statue.
- Lady Liberty wears a size 879 shoe.
- A broken shackle and chains lies at her feet.
- Two images of the torch are on the ten-dollar bill.
- Lady Liberty's face was modeled after Bartholdi's mother!

National Monument

VISITORS

The Statue of Liberty is a national monument.
A national monument is an important place
protected by the federal government.
It is set aside for the American people to enjoy!

You can visit the Statue of Liberty.
First, you can explore the museum in the pedestal.
Then, you can climb all the way up to the crown!
That's 354 steps, so you had better be in good shape!

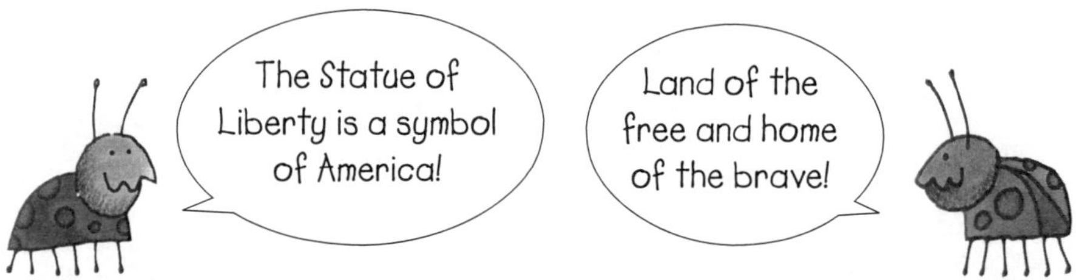

GLOSSARY

centennial: a 100th anniversary or its celebration

engineer: a person who designs or builds machines and structures like bridges, buildings, or roads

framework: an essential supporting structure of a building, vehicle, or object

immigrant: a person who comes to live permanently in a foreign country

monument: a structure or building built to honor a special person or event

pedestal: a support or base for a column or statue

plaque: a wood or metal tablet attached to a wall to remember a person or event

shackle: a metal ring used to secure a person's wrists or ankles